Stories of a Polished Pistil

Lace and Ruffles

Maquita Donyel Irvin

Stories of a Polished Pistil

Lace and Ruffles

Maquita Donyel Irvin

DEDICATION

Thank you to those that have supported, encouraged,
and loved me along the way.
A special thank you to God, my lovely mother,
and my remarkable daughter.
Mom, smooches.
Mini, zucchini infinity.

So often she was told that her emotions were too deep, her smile too
friendly, and/or her dreams too big.
She was *too quiet* when she should be loud and *too loud* when she ought
to be quiet.
Too, *too*, much of her.

This is for her,
This is for me,
This is for you.

You cannot ever be too much of yourself.

Don't fear it, don't mask it, feel it. Fall madly in love with it; all of it.
Its beauty, its flaws, its simplicity, its intricacy, its entire being.

Share it. Spread it.
Ask God to sharpen it, but by no means allow the opinions of others to
change it.

You're not too deep, you don't love too hard.
Truth is, your refusal to become the woman they want you to be, your
insistence on becoming the woman God wants you to be, scares the crap
out of them.
So they will discourage it and you will fight it.
Fight it beautifully, elegantly, loudly, or quietly.
However God has told you is best to fight your fight, fight it.

Polished Pistil™?
It's our fight, our life, our voice, our stories, our ups, our downs, our
songs, our glory.
These are our stories.
It's proof that you're not alone. It's proof that we are in it together.

-Maquita Donyel

CONTENTS

AUTHOR'S NOTE

Stories of a Polished Pistil is a collection of poems and short stories compiled into three characters: Kair, Bon, and Scarlette. It covers their beautiful highs, deep lows, and some of the misters they encountered along the way.

You will read their *pieces*, a collection of poems related to them and you will read their *songs*, short stories that provide further insight into each character.

Every poem is titled with a number, every short story is titled with a number and a name.

KAIR

You are disarmingly beautiful, yet humble. You're down to earth in a girl next door kind of way. This is rare. — A Mister

Kair's Pieces

0.1 Mister

This book was not written for you.

This book was not written for you to sit back and reminisce
on all of our good and bad instances.

If anything, simply marvel at its existence.

Feel it deeply

allow it to run through your veins

and when it starts to cause pain, run your tongue down it.

And when the pages manage to slit open a piece of your skin,
choose to love it anyway.

0.2
She wasn't Carrie nor Charlotte, Whitley nor Denise
She was a combination of them all
A concoction that no man or woman could procreate
Unseen, unheard, not yet felt
A heart made of hues not learned in school
But of hues millions could relate to if they took a second or two
Easy to lust
Easy to love
Difficult to unriddle

0.3 Worthy

It's time we terminate guilting and shaming and crediting
ourselves with damage that we did not choose to create alone
For unmade and made beds that were not only our own
For critiquing and disparaging our most powerful, earth
shattering tool... love.
There's no shame in love.
There's no shame in loving, feeling, fighting and caring for
another human being.
There's no shame in being woman, in being unforgivingly and
forcefully magnificent.

0.4 Why

She writes to live it once

And taste it twice

To pass it once to the left so they can taste it thrice

To feel it intensely

And attempt to provide a bit of insight

Into what it is like to be the

Thick

Messy

Vibrant

Flesh, blood, fire, and bones sitting under a perfectly, imperfect,

Purposefully molded face.

She writes to make sense of this space and all the complexity that

Fills it.

0.5 How

Chasing down elusive thoughts
her cheeks warmed over in joy

Leading to emotions without words
emotions that forewarned a stomach joyfully torn
blissfully leaping through metaphors
while holding tightly to the colorful words buried deeply in her
pocket
These words were more valuable than gold

These words allowed her to express herself in ways untold
ways she otherwise would have never told

Like the time she survived recurring rainstorms
only to be weighed down in a reign storm
where crowns were won
crowns were worn
and eventually lost

Or the time love was made
against all odds
and da da dees
and da da doos
and ma ma mees
and la la loos
were the only way she could sensibly explain
what it felt like to love
what it felt like to write
what it felt like to get lost in a synonym hunt for words other than
"da dees, da doos, ma mees, la loos"

0.6 Lyf
I didn't come looking for you
the day you uninvitedly appeared on my doorstep

How did we go from a nonchalant conversation
me waiting for you to turn me off
with corny jokes and mind dumbing conversation
to
love

To love and mind blowing chemistry that I've yet to make sense of
What are you here to teach me?

0.7
It's obvious in every conversation
and in every deflected emotion and statement
that God created us from the same part of earth.
How did we end up on opposite sides of it?

0.8

Ah, so this is how one loves again
To be ok with all that lies within despite what harry, joan, or sue
thought of it
What tony thought of it,
What deShawn thought of it
What one's boss, mom, auntie, or cousin thought of it.
So this is what it's like to celebrate her and all that her garden was
created to be.
God was unapologetic when he created her,
so it's time she save her sorrys.

0.9 Backspace
Clearing the history you and I created
Would be like deleting years of written works
Years of a mysterious, contagious, illogical, and forbidden love
Deleting our history would mean deleting you
Parts of me
Parts of us
And well, we owe the world more than that

1.0

Denying the beauty of one's love escapade simply because it was
not meant to last forever would be denying one's growth and
potentially one's very existence
It would mean denying that an intentional and purposeful part of
time and space existed
Permanence isn't always Love's goal
Sometimes Love's goal is growth;
character shaking, rebuilding, and reshaping kind of growth
Sometimes Love's goal is to expose you to a world worth loving
Sometimes Love comes along just to bring you up and out of a pit
of hell disguised as love
and when you're up and out of it
that particular Love's mission is complete

My Dear,
You mustn't trivialize a love that has departed simply because its
mission is over and its time is up
You also mustn't guilt, force, cry, and/or beg for it to stay past its
assigned departure date
You needed one another for reasons that may infinitely go
unknown to the both of you,
find peace in that
Simply be thankful that it ever came and extended a hand
Be thankful that it left just in time for you to continue your
journey towards another Love;
one within yourself,
one for others,
and one for another
more fitting
Love.

1.1

She thanked him for letting go
Letting go of a queen destined for a king,
For not letting her fall too deep
For not leading her down their passionate sea of troubled waters
For breaking her fall as she began to fall far too deeply in love
With him

1.2 New Habits

How does one learn overnight to live a life that hasn't been lived
for six revolutions around the sun?

How does one learn how to start accepting our now, our today,
and our potential tomorrows,

all of which include

you

and

I

but separately.

Song Bird 1.3
Just keep her strong.
Lord, just keep her unafraid to sing the song placed in the pit of
her heart.

1.4 Gratitude

By the age of 8 I had it all figured out.
What color I'd wear
who'd be my bridesmaids
who'd be there to see me and he
make a commitment before He.
Headed down the road of suburban picnics
white picket fences
little versions of me and he
the size of a soccer team

Devastating.

Devastating how close I was to living in a world of naivety
In a world fighting for its spirituality
in a world so mean
in a world full of beauty deeper than any idea of perfection could
reach.
I was six steps away from being sucked into eternity
with the wrong he and his white picket fences
more like a cage for a woman like me
not reaching what I was destined to reach.

Thank God for the grass so green and the grass so brown,
thank God for the beauty found in different backgrounds.

Thank God for the minds not chained to dollar signs.

Thank God for colored fences, dull fences, jagged fences,
and fences that refuse to be called fences.
For handsome fellas with stories that go deeper than privilege,
or excuses,
or resentment,
and for the ladies brave enough to love again.

Thank God for different
and thank God for not having it all figured out.

1.5 Encourager

On her back were many stories untold

Wisdom from the too young and too old

Secrets carefully stored and dreams told

An iron spine that

Only faith and grace could mold

Each night she held a light

For the dreamers of the day

And those of the night

And for each tear any queen had ever cried

1.6 Stained Roots

I woke up in a sweat
I fell asleep and had a dream that a king
A king I had known since the day he was visibly growing within
The comforting walls of his queen.
I feel asleep and had a dream that this king was liquidated by a
Group of kind faces.
You know, the kind faces beautifully outlined in our elusive
History books.
The books that omitted things like, "Lift every voice and sing"
And the faces that sang them,
For the voices of the fathers of this great, great, nation
Of takers, enslavers, murders, and hatred.
The kind faces that this nation has taught us all to aspire to be
The faces that I love, genuinely love
But do not wish to be.
I woke up in a sweat,
In a pool as wet as this king's shirt after the bullet impermissibly
Broke his royal, purposeful, nurturing brown skin
I woke up in a sweat as burning as his queens fears
And as fearful as his little king's tears.
I woke up in a pool of tears burning red and white stripes down
My face, stars in my eyes, stars that I've been taught by society to
Hide unless the coincide with whether or not society has deemed
Them worth sharing
For the sake of being too ethnic, or black, exotic, or racy.
I woke up with the blood of that king covering my kind walls
My privileged walls,
My privileged sheets.
It's been 115 bodies, I mean nights
It's been 115 nights and counting that this dream has come to me
How does one find rest in this reoccurring theme?
This is anything but a dream

1.7 Birthright

Sometimes when she's discouraged

She thinks of the blood

The blood on the cross

The blood that flowed through the veins of her ancestors

And how that very same blood is the blood that runs through her.

She thinks of how strong that blood must have been to get her

Here today.

For that reason alone,

She mustn't give up.

1.8 Bloom
She was completely whole
And yet never fully complete

Father 1.9
Bring me to my knees
Create a Love in me
One that surpasses all understanding
Mold me and place my feet on the lapis lazuli promised to me
Humble me
With all of You.

2.0
But with Him, she can do it
But with Him, she's going to do it
But with Him, she's doing it.

2.1 Crown Her

If she said she didn't want to shake it
she was lying
If she said she didn't practice in the mirror
she was lying
If she said she didn't feel it every time he grabbed her by the hand
or took a stand against the man
she was lying

So why lie
about who she was created to be
about what lies between her thighs and its immaculate beauty
She is Women,
designed to create, love, and teach
to make love and reach levels and peaks no one knew could be
reached

Not just with any man walking
but the one that deserved she
the one that prayed for she
the one brave enough to fight for her and get down on one knee
the one that made a vow before God
that her heart he'd protect and keep

She's a prize
a prize that any eyes could see
shamelessly sexy, shamelessly free
Because what's truly captivating
What truly makes her free?

My dear, this goes deeper than what any eyes can see
It's felt deeply and undeniably
not through the ability to make his knees feel weak, under satin
sheets, over 90s r&b beats
but in her ability to limit her availability
and carefully choose who she allowed entry
Because in a world that promotes freedom as promiscuity
and overexposure and lack of privacy
She found freedom in saving herself for Him, for her,
and her future he,
Celibacy.

2.2 Today
She refused to fall victim to the belief
that honoring her body meant being a tease,
giving just a little piece, or welcoming one of many encounters
providing access to her soul with ease.
Even if yesterday she said 'yes'
today and everyday going forward
she took pleasure in saying, 'no.'

2.3 Blessing | Curse
Suddenly, with just a glance into his eyes
she could see past his bright smile,
over his beautiful words,
and into the corners of his soul.
Unable to be persuaded by the exterior.

2.4
he said,
"The world you live in has no place for me.
Life isn't butterflies sitting side by side swinging on wooden swings.
It isn't sweet songs sung over virgin drinks in a hot, summer breeze."

She simply replied,
"Why can't it be?"

2.5
She just believed there was more
to life than
finding ways to escape it

2.6
Rare and far between
A mind coated with colorful skies, tall trees, strong branches
With attached wooden swings
Butterflies would sing
In fact, things were really green until they were really blue
A complex soul dealt a plethora of unidentifiable hues

When diving into the ocean of vulnerability,
She swam nude
Or at least hoped to

But along with the fish of love and light
Swam fish of hurt and truth;
They'd bite
And the starfish of the sea? So externally bright
Would viciously pierce her skin

But never would she do away with them
She simply used their points and teeth
To pin her curls in, under and back
Because thanks to them she now had tougher skin and brighter
eyes
She understood that messy hands didn't earn her a lesser life

She believed in true love, true friendships, and oversized dreams
In encouraging Pistils to develop their petals
And angels to find their wings

Believed in pushing through dry spells in the winter
And severe storms every summer-eve

The daughter of a queen
That preferred Gospel with her gin
And Hip Hop with her tea

2.7 Faint-of-Heart

Her words exposed him to feelings he never knew existed
while her presence effortlessly disarmed what he'd been
protecting for years
he knew that if he'd explore any further
he'd love her
they'd all love her
and he'd never want to leave
so, he left

2.8 The slip up
If only
she would stop dragging in what wants to go
needs to go
and has no business
lounging on her doorstep

2.9 Dear Diary

I met another you
Well-spoken, yet slightly clumsy with his words like you
Well-mannered yet mysterious like you
I always said, "I'd never again mistakenly be with you.
I'd never again be drawn in by you"

But there he was, with just enough cool
Plotting on how to lead my thoughts down and through
The very same captivating melodic loop

You'd pick me up just to later pin me down
Simply because you liked the sound of my growl
Colorful promises and instant regrets
All of which eventually I longed to have

he sought me out like he met me before
Like he knew my heart had just been washed to shore

Just like then, like us in that store in twenty-ten
I grinned, flirted back, and concluded with witty statements

But unlike then, I saw the trap
Left him there, left you there, without a single look back

Conclusion?
As an attempt to be clear and not *long-winded*
I'm glad it ended.

3.0 Decamp

She escaped beneath the grey and blue sky of his and hers
dreams, aspirations, fears
his and hers tears
it only took five years.

Running into a wilderness of confused thoughts
and thoughts of, "Where do I go from here?"
Hoping that once she arrives she can only go up.
That the light she once had
will peak through the beautiful branches of deceit and over the
fence guarding her heart.

That her dreams are still carved in that handmade swing,
the place she loved most to be.
Hoping that it would still whimsically swing from the tree that He
and she grew together through unfathomable weather,
emotions, and times.
Hoping the roots were rooted deep enough to come back to.

Leaving behind all that she'd ever hoped from him
and never was.
Her heart, although cracked, still beating
heavy breathing, sobbing
running with his heart beneath her feet
wind beneath her hair and just enough hope in her piercing,
brown eyes.
Leaving the idea,
welcoming the reality,
retreating to a new beginning.

3.1 Floating

Surrounded by a sea of waves, moving at no particular pace
Rocking back and forth, to and away from you and the broken
Groundwork we've laid
Just me, you, and oceans of space
Lots of space
Waiting for the stars to arrive and fill our empty space

Mostly alive, but now somewhat numb to you
A boat full of empty promises will do that to you

Not caring if I were to drift away
Into new waters escorted by a new handsome face
There I could build a home on stable ground, if I were to drift
It'd be ok because the waters would be safe underneath,
Under morning satin sheets
Under yummy days and mini bites to eat.

3.2 Gems

Sometimes she found that she gave more credit to the scars
Than she gave to the healer and those that assisted in the healing
She acknowledged the darkness
When the stars were the ones that brought her out of it
What about the stars?
It was time to acknowledge them.

I just want to lay up with your spirit;
with all that makes you, you. — A Mister

3.3
Don't fight it
Delight in her desire to win,
How she leaves your demons with nothing left to defend
While quite complex for one to comprehend
Go with her

<u>Kair's Song</u>

1.0 Paint and Ruffles

The day started just like an ordinary summer day

1. Thanking God to be awake
2. A rushed coffee break
3. A talk with mom to jump start her day

A whimsical rush out the door
Today would be anything but a bore
Texts between girlfriends confirming the plans drawn up the
Night before

As she made it back home from work,
And the daunting tasks of choosing an outfit began to lurk
She grabbed her dress
And did a little twerk

Comfort never failed and neither did a red lip
In her comfy black coned shoes
She pulled off in her whip

An hour late, some called it fate
She'd call it poor planning for a date
Parking garage was $10 for only a short hour
"Be back at 11 pm or they're going to close the gate"

Off rushed Cinderella
Under her white ruffled umbrella
Past a slew of dolled up ladies with their fellas

She found her girl at the front door
Waiting on the second floor
Neither had been there before

Finally inside
And to her surprise
People were packed wall to wall

Pancakes, booze, a DJ with tattoos
Someone live painting on somebody's boobs

They mingled and danced
Her other girls joined them at last
And they had nothing short of an absolute blast

Her time was almost up,
So she finished her cup,
And began to look for her keys.
Just when she thought her night was over,
She looked up and over and heard him say, "Excuse me, please."

"I've seen you quite a bit," said she.
"Have you seen my work?" replied he.
"No, I haven't"
 "Come with me"

But it was 10:46 and her car was a block away
But what the heck,
he was cute and she wanted to see this display

6'5 at least
he offered a drink
And they had a bit of chat and chit
he fed her weakness for intelligent communication,
Undivided attention and dope acrylics

"Nice to meet you," she said, "but I have to go"
"May I have your number? I can't forget you, yo."
He hugged her a few times, she ran her hand across his neck
The girls made it to her car with two minutes to spare

It was all quite magical
Because she had forgotten what it was like
To feel so giddy
So high
So light

Their story ended there
But don't you fear
This brief meeting fulfilled a purpose indeed
You see
She'd almost given in
To the sensible man to marry
The one with the good job, sense of humor, and lots of money
She forgot how much she appreciated those crazy tummy fairies

Every butterfly you meet
Won't be the one you need
But if you allow it, they'll lead you closer to where you're
Supposed to be
Because shortly after he
Came
Love.

Kair's Pieces

3.4 Mama Wisdom
"Honey, it's not that you aren't ready," she said
"It's that you just haven't met the right one
And you're not ready to settle for the wrong one."

3.5
She was rare, few and far between
She suspected he would be as well
And the thought of two rare, few and far between individuals
Doing all that was necessary for that rare, few and far between
Meeting to occur
Drove her to write

3.6 The Right One
A seed was planted the day they crossed paths
The day his hand accidently brushed against hers
In the intersection of
I'm ready and I'm not sure yet
Maybe someday they'll water it

3.7
In the mood for Love songs
over wine pours
and unforced dialect about Him
with you

3.8 Sister, Brother, Lover, Kin
The art
buried deeply
within me
is thankful
for the art
oozing out of you.

3.9 Hunger
he loved her mind
But she needed him to love her soul
Feed her spirit
And love her whole

4.0 Him, Capital H
I don't care to be the one you need
I simply care to be the woman He's called me to be
And if consequently that leads you flowing towards me
Don't hold back
Let go
Just let us be

4.1
Got her over thinking and over speaking
Suddenly motivated
But steady dreaming
She should've been more careful
More careful with her prayers
Now there's no going back
No unseeing what they shared
And that load is heavy

4.2 The Big Things

She really liked old beats
New beats, worn seats, and old coffee shops
She liked the feeling she got when the beat would drop
Long shirts
Short skirts
Laughs and true love
How looking into the eyes of another could make the world stop
How He made her world stop and repeatedly gave her another
Shot
For He so loved the world

4.3 What Changed?

The belief that she deserved half

Half of it, half of them, half of her, half of him

What changed was the disbelief that she deserved anything less than all.

She chose to make herself courageously available to all that God had for her.

As for her fears?

They would have wait.

4.4 Faith Driven

With only her feet on solid ground
She longed to sail among the wind of purpose
Unafraid of where His path may take her
Gracefully embracing the ride
Whether it be whimsical or jarring
Finding beauty in every moment
In every encounter
In every place

<u>Bon</u>

You have this calming presence about you. You have a
voice that instantly soothes the soul.-A mister

Bon's Pieces

0.1 Sweet Fire
Her presence? Magic.
The depths of her thoughts will have you never wanting to
surface for air
When she spoke of the dreams in her heart, fireflies danced in her
eyes,
dreams larger than ones he could ever imagine.
She was his sweet little escape. High yet completely sober
left with traces of her olive branch skin and memories of jasmine
between the coils of hair.
Each soul touched was left with a firefly of their own buried deep
within their hearts, untouched, unmatched, undying.

0.2
When you find it
Others will indeed be drawn to it
They will fawn over it
Fall in love with it
Request more of it just for themselves
And while this may temporarily cause it to grow brighter
You must remember not to fall dependent
Because when the external admiration is gone
What will remain is the beautiful person that ignited it
And the King that created it.
Never lose sight of her, never forget Him

0.3 Rein, Reign, Rain
Fantasy like thoughts that no man could rein
Just let her reign
Run wild with her unafraid
Of any rain storms
They only wash the mud away and make way
For double rainbows and sunny days

0.4 Hopeful Romantic

Blame it on the stars
Her thoughts hardly stopped
Jumping city to city
Planet to planet
From Like to Love
For Love
Was her favorite place to be
The food tasted best there
The tingles down her spine
Felt at home there
The skirts twirled and all words said held true, there.
Fear? Less.
Beauty? Full and overflowing from the inside out
Every hand reaching to help another
Bellies aching from the joyful stories shared.
After seeking He
She found herself
She found him there
Working his life away waiting
For the day
She'd walk by
he'd say hi
Love would be there

0.5 Old Souls Young Hearts
Go away with me
pick a day
to heat up a cold place
or liven up the middle of June
dancing to tunes from the 70s

Run away with me from the city lights
away from road rage fights and overnight flights
let's sway in the breeze,
sing off key
find an underground spot to vibe to reggae beats

Hide away with me
behind the morning sun
they say the night is young
but with me the day is better
effortlessly capturing the organ that lies behind that navy blue
sweater
good girls do it better
all I need is twenty four

Bon's Song

1.0 The First

March 2015:
(The 'I'm Done' Text)

Bon sends a text at 1:32AM:

"Adonis, the love will always be there. A love like ours doesn't die. We fell in love purely and innocently but it's been ten years. Ten years of me watching you seek versions of me. Ten years of listening to you unknowingly compare them to me and hearing how you'd call out my name in their presence. Ten years of you comparing them to us.

There isn't another me. There will not be another us and I'm done watching you subconsciously torture yourself over that reality. I'm done allowing it to torture me. I love you, but you're selfish...and well, it's time that I choose me.

I do hope that eventually you run full force into all that God has for you. That you stop allowing your fears and your insecurities to dictate your story. That you become the amazing man I've always believed you will become. Not for me, but for God, for your daughter, for your family, and for yourself. While 'The never ending story of Adonis on Bon,' may live on, this chapter, the one that includes you and me together...will not. Goodbye Donnie. I love you."

April 2006:
(The Heartbreak)

I opened the door.

"He cheated, Kair," Bon sobbed as she stumbled into my doorway. Her knees collapsed, her purse fell to the floor, and her entire body sank into mine. "Adonis cheated."

"Let's go upstairs before my mom hears you," I said.

We've been friends since we were eight; Bon, Scarlette and I.

During this particular incident, we were seventeen. It was a month before prom and the guy we all thought Bon would marry *practically* cheated on her. I say *practically* because technically, the sexual encounter happened a few hours after Bon and Adonis split. I hadn't ever seen Bon so distraught; not even during her parent's nasty divorce.

You see, Bon is the air of the group.
She walks as if clouds were beneath her feet. If you stared at her long enough, you could almost see the wind playing hopscotch between the strands of her hair. Even her voice was soft and sweet; think Thandie Newton without the British accent. Although, Bon could fake a good British accent.

Bon and Adonis had been split up for less than 24 hours and Scarlette, the other piece to our puzzle, called to tell her that Adonis, the love of Bon's life, had slept with her "friend." I say "friend" because Bon didn't know her well. So, let's call her Foe.

Bon was the type of girl that wanted everyone to feel included, especially the excluded. Foe was an insecure girl from a nearby city and knew Bon for all of six months. Little did we know, "this" (you know, sleeping with someone else's man type of "this") was the type of thing Foe did regularly.

As for Adonis? Simply put, it was a punk ass move. A move that, as her best friend, I'll help her forgive and I'll even help her forget, but *I* won't forget. I won't forget how hard it was for her to end it with him. I won't forget how instead of putting his pride aside, grabbing her by the hand, and pulling her out of the hole he helped get her in, he pushed her further in it. All he had to do was be there. All he had to do was hear her, hold her, and love her. But instead, he stepped on her chest and didn't let up. He left her gasping for air; and at seventeen? For life.

(Let's Rewind Again)
July 2005:
(The First Time Bon and Adonis Met)

"Kair, I met a guy. Well, I met him online. We're supposed to meet this afternoon while my mom is gone. In case he turns out to be some 40 year old creep that prays on sweet little girls like me, you need to know where we're meeting, what time, and what kind of car he's driving," said Bon.

"First, you're not sweet. Second," Kair sighed, "Bon, what have you got us into?"
"Make sure you send me his license plate number. I'll call you in five minutes. If everything is ok say, "5 stars" and if it's not say, "1 star." I'll have the cops there before you can say..."

"Okay, okay I'll let you know when he's here," Bon interrupted.

In hindsight, we could've crafted better code words. We could've crafted a better plan altogether. Like, why in the heck was she meeting a guy online at 16?! I digress.

At 12:00 in the afternoon Adonis put on a fitted cap, a black LRG tee, and basketball shorts to head to Bon's home.

They were from opposite sides of the bridge. Being from opposite sides of the bridge was like being from opposite sides of the world, although only 20 minutes apart.

They were the classic Romeo and Juliet story except their parents were equally excited about them being together. Sooo more like Martin and Gina from the Martin Lawrence Show, or Whitley and Dwayne from A Different World. They were polar opposites and yet, somehow perfect for each other.

She was an undeniably, beautiful, free spirited Northern VA preacher's kid slightly obsessed with Maroon 5 and Lil Wayne. He was, *that* guy. That aesthetically pleasing, over six feet tall, basketball playing, most popular kid in school, guy. He didn't really know it though; the absence of his father weighed heavily on his confidence and sense of direction. They had that in common; both belonging to strong, hardworking, single mothers and both figuring out how to deal with the unintentional rejection from their fathers.

He pulled up in a 2-door hatchback Honda Civic finished with black rims, a speaker system, illegal tents, and a New Car air freshener hanging in his window. He reached into his pocket, grabbed his phone, flipped it open, and called Bon to let her know he was downstairs.

"Okay I'll be down" said Bon.
Nervous as all get out, Bon left her house, locked the door, walked down the hall and pressed the down button for the elevator.

She texted:
"Kair, he's here. I'll send you the license plate number in a bit."

The elevator arrived.

She got into the elevator wearing her blue Seven jeans, white tank top, and checkered Converses. Her hair was gelled back into a slick pony tail. She nervously played with her Tiffany's bracelet as the elevator headed down to the first floor.

She got out of the elevator, walked past her building's convenience store, and out of the glass doors.
 "Here we go," she said under her breath.
She saw the car Adonis described in a previous conversation parked just outside of the front door; a 2-door hatchback Honda Civic. She took a glimpse of the Maryland license plate and sent

the tag number to Kair. She opened the car door and there he was.
He was more beautiful than the pictures online. Fresh haircut,
hazel eyes, caramel skin, and cheeks covered in freckles.
He hadn't seen a girl quite like her before.
Bon, however was very good at pretending she wasn't nervous.
"Hey," she said casually with a grin and got into the car.
They hugged.
"Where do you want to go?" Adonis asked.
"Umm, let's just go to the parking lot down the street."

They parked just down the hill from her home and talked
…and talked
…and talked for hours.

The attraction was indescribable and the connection was
uncommon. She played with her hair as she told him old stories
and he was unable to hide his laughs. The two of them, revealed
things they hadn't revealed to anyone else before.

After their first meeting came amusement park dates, basketball
games, meeting the parents, family cookouts, meeting the entire
family, awkward conversations about protecting themselves (in
case they chose to have sex), and Sunday night football and/or
board games at his mother's house. Perfection beyond
comprehension. So perfect that well, we all envied them.

Bon had finally met her match. As for Adonis? This was the first
time he knew what it was like to want to spend the rest of his life
with a girl.

Bon's Pieces

0.6 In the mood

In the mood to hit snooze
and cuddle under you
easing your every worry
Don't let go
let's watch the sunrise
don't get up
let's make the bed rise
don't give up
baby it's you and I.
I rise up
and feed your appetite
with promises to never leave your side
and standards I'd never compromise
like no one has made you feel inside.
The power of the mind.

0.7 Blue Jeans

Remember the time we left certainty behind
For sunny days in California?
Laid on the beach
Sharing space and dreams
Remember the time I stole your jeans
And covered them with yellow and red beads?
Still waiting on your to forgive me
For stealing
Dismantling
For leaving indestructible traces of me
On your soul
On your mind
On your favorite piece
On your favorite pair of blue jeans

Bon's Song

1.0 The First, continued...

"We were both my favorite and least favorite, love story"
— A Polished Pistil

Spring came and things started to shift. As her college acceptance letters began to come in, he felt her slipping away. A slew of broken promises from him, arguments started by her, and dark clouds they never knew existed soon hovered over their relationship with no sign of dispersing.
He recognized a light in Bon that she hadn't yet recognized in herself. He knew that if she were to go away to college while in a relationship with him, it would hold her back. He didn't want to hold her back and he didn't want to take any chances of getting hurt.

April 2006:
(The Breakup)

"My friend thinks we should take a break," Adonis said to Bon.

Bon drove to his house after her part-time waitressing job. She parked in her usual spot on the side of the house and snuck in through the basement door.

There they sat at 11:30 PM on his bed. They were upset, utterly confused, and unsure of how they got to such a dark place. Neither of them wanting to let go but so full of pride, they wouldn't admit it. So, they let go.

"Who the hell is your friend, Adonis? And why are you talking to a chick I don't know, or ANY chick for that matter, about OUR relationship? OF COURSE she's going to tell you to take a break.

People hate us together. AND you listened?! So, clearly I'm not as important to you as you say. I don't do breaks Adonis, we're done." And so they were done.

April 2006
(1.5 Days Later)

I opened the door, she sank, she cried, and I watched a little piece of her leave with him.

"Scar, you have to come over...," I texted Scarlette.

Scarlette came over. We cried, we prayed, we cried some more, and we pigged out on chips and salsa.

"You promise I'll be alright?" Bon asked.
"Love, you'll be better than all right," I responded.
"Better than you ever imagined," added Scar.
Adonis and Bon went one year without speaking. She had since moved away to college, met a guy, left a guy, and vowed to be single for a while. Adonis had since joined the military and began dating someone else. They caught up again, they talked about the day he cheated, and emotions resurfaced. He asked her for love advice, she provided it, she asked him for love advice, he provided it. Then, they argued and they went another 1.5 years without speaking. During that time she met another man and had a baby. He met another woman, married her, and had a baby as well.
Nonetheless, as fate would have it, Adonis and Bon's paths would cross again.

To be continued...

Bon's Pieces

0.8 Me.Us.Then
Poor fellah,
You simply made the mistake of thinking every woman after me
would be like me
Weeks, after years,
after weeks and weeks
All that came after me
unable to know you
without knowing a piece of me
It's ok to delight in the random traces of me
just don't seek another woman like me
just stop hoping for another me
another then
another us

0.9 Hazel

I was told by a sweet soul
A wise soul, one that you know far more than I,
That although we ended today
We may not end forever.
It told me not to count you out,
Not to count us out,
It told me not to count out the possibility of you and I and
My, oh my.
Well, that could be why.
That could be why although I was 100 percent sure
In my very sure soul
That although my indifference could be felt from the
Tippy top tip of my hair follicle
Down to the tippy top tip of my big toe,
That although I was through with us
We were unable to fully disconnect.
The moment those words were spoken,
The moment that innocent declaration was made aloud in the very
Air you and I took deep, intimate, breaths in
Our lunges were filled with it.
It filled our lungs, penetrated our hearts, and ran through our
Young, helpless veins.
This is possibly the reason why although I never wished to
Connect again in that way,
My heart still tugged when you pained,
My heart still tugged for joy when you would celebrate.
It is possibly the reason why my heart tried to throw itself over a
Bridge at the mention of your name.
Why in places without a single trace of me, you subconsciously
Searched for my name…hoping to see…hoping to feel my name.
It is possibly the reason you, we, were never the same.

1.0 Forewarning
That was then
The time is new
Just us belonging to
Two different two
Never again me and you

.

.

.

Never again
Me
And
You

Scarlette

Listen little mama, you and I both know that you're a stone cold fox and you never had a brother you couldn't do without. —A mister

<u>Scarlette's Song</u>

1.0 Invisible Scar(s)

he was hurt, but did everything in his power to appear otherwise.
At this point he figured that the only way to survive is through causing
hurt to others; causing hurt to her.
To him love meant to control. he *loved* her, so he kept her confined to his
space.
A space that would at first appear safe,
full of grace, and true love.
But it was a space that would soon leave her inaccessible to the world
and left with him.
The type of him she swore she would never entertain
he told her he loved her but thought loving her meant containing her
That it meant making her feel helpless without him
Because to him he was protecting what he had once lost
and refused to lose again.
"Yes you're trapped but within this trap is a little white space. Aren't you
grateful for your white space?! Why aren't you grateful for your white
space?!" he exclaimed.
he was hurt
But to him it wasn't't hurt at all
Nah, it wasn't pain,
he shifted blame
Everything wrong in his life was due to Leona, Sam, and Jane
B/c through them, he saw her
The first her that he'd ever know
She birthed him and it was she that left him alone
Walked out of his life
and he hurt.
he'd never admit it though
So hurt, he remained.
And now hurt she remained
Years she would spend
trying to break free
from the scars of abuse
discounted because it wasn't done physically

Scarlette's Pieces

0.1 Runaway
Her peace
She lost it
Back between the cracks of a busy road
In between the grey leather seats of bitterness
and up and through the roof top of broken promises
It's a wonder how she ever had it
Ever found it
Ever shared it
Someone with a story like hers
You'd think never had it
Her life was a gift without the big red velvet bow
But a bow made of twine, lace, tears and barb wire instead
Thorns, flower petals, and soft kisses held it together.
Prayer held her together.
So long as she didn't allow herself to lose her peace to him, it or
Them

0.2 Unconditional

After the white canvas has been covered
After the colors painted and sprayed have faded away
When her smile not be bright
And her light too afraid to reveal its cracks
Love her
Love her in her messiest state

0.3 Intentionally Accidental
We were different colors
On different paths
Colliding at what seemed by chance
Over and over again

0.4 Gift of Gab Habit

Beards and brushes
Were her favorite
They knew it
They'd clumsily talk their way into her mind
Easing past the iron walls surrounding her heart
With talks of purpose, and God, and light, and dreams
And love,
But not playing for keeps
They'd paint a picture of her soul
Parts that only she should know
They'd be there only when she'd be ready for them to go
And only after a melodramatic show
Featuring kisses on ear lobes
Would they go

0.5

She had a power within
A power that could reveal light in even the most dim of men
And inadvertently make herself their new addiction
Inadvertently make them fall in
Her well of glory, love and hopelessness in search of hopefulness

0.6 Glutton for Pain (t)
She was 18
he, immature, insecure but practically pure
he loved her
Too fast
Too much
Too sweet
Simply put, she wasn't ready
And he wasn't ready
Unaware of her power she recklessly swung it around
Two dates later using it to unsystematically capture his heart
Nine years later it has yet to come loose
And instead of letting go
he held on, overwhelmed by subconscious anguish,
Pulled apart by insecure thoughts of "Why not me? Why him? If only she
could see me for who I really am."

Little did she know she broke his heart

Little did she know he never forgave her
Little did she know that after those very few dates
every attempt to contact her going forward would be a subconscious
attempt to ruin her
Not to love her or lift her
But to paint her soul with the dark colors he'd been saving just for her
Planning to then let her loose into the world headed down an emotional
whirlwind feeling defeated

Little did she know he'd become an artist

Every couple of years she'd run away
he'd pull her back with random check-ins
Stories about how it didn't work out with his most recent girlfriend
She thought it would be safe to let him in
Daddy issues caused her to idolize those that at least came back in
She'd think, 'at least he's a good friend'
Soon enough she'd allow his brushes to penetrate her skin
Colors that were once so bright had started to become dim

Stories of a Polished Pistil: Lace and Ruffles

Using name-calling and critiques as a weapon, as a way to keep her under
him
Subconsciously, strapped around his leaking, wounded heart were notes
taken over the years on how to defeat her

"If I can't have her, she can't win."

Refusing to truly show his heart and yet demanding to see, feel and
touch every part of hers
And every attempt he made to get in
she welcomed him in

She forgave
and she forgot
and she replaced each memory of attempted core murder
with thoughts of 'what if'
'could be'
and 'he didn't mean it'
Choosing potential over reality

And with every ounce of darkness he threw at her she returned with
light

But now he was winning
And through tears, fears, and overrun (and overdone) thoughts
she prayed
"Something's not right. It must be me," she'd say
she'd run away
To clear up some mental space
he'd pull her back
She'd come back
Nearly covered in black paint
She'd let him pin her up against his wall

"You're a glutton for paint, huh girl?"
Glutton for pain
Glutton for wishing on better days

0.7 Astute
Like a lion on a wildebeest
Offering a shoulder to place her seas of sorrows
Not knowing they would ultimately drown his ulterior wishes
To depths of no return.
Don't dare come for her heart with ill intention
Nor for her soul without permission
She's no victim, my love.

0.8 Baby She Wolf
She'll walk near the white line, she'll even walk on top of it
but if you dare push, ask, or in any way cause her to walk over it
she'll swallow you whole
leaving only your heart
walking and fully exposed
with her name etched into its edges
letting everyone know you came
you loved
you crossed

Fragmented 0.9
She pulled and pushed
Heart never content
So fascinated by the broken
That her disbelief of self
Led to unrealistic beliefs in others
"But I'm a good person," she cried,
"Why do so many hurt me?"
As she nibbled on the broken hearted and empty
The broken feast on the broken

1.0 Stained Glass

Look deeply into her eyes
Past the inevitable wounds she
Encountered along the way
Warming the ice cold barrier with a pure heart,
A deeply felt touch and an attentive ear.
Listen carefully to the beats of her heart and
The whispers of her soul
Accept it all.
Don't let go.

1.1 Progress
Somehow ending up in a place where she loved how everything
flowed
Where even she glowed from the inside out
Nourished seeds were sewed
Laughs on a regular basis with those she loved
Love
She could love all day
But, towards him
She found guards at every corner of her heart
There to protect her from the rulers of its past

1.2 Prince Charming

All things beautiful aren't gold
Or even safe to hold dear to your heart for that matter
Especially when they aren't yours to hold
Some things that are beautiful must be let go
And told never to return again
Because the beauty that once healed you could ultimately end in
Annihilation
And there's no remedy for the passion that stems from this sort of
Self-destruction.
There's no water deep enough to drown that fire
It'll simply grow higher and higher
Beautifully suffocating everything in the room
And everything attached to it
Including you.
Gotta know when a stage is through
Gotta see it through

1.3 medicine man
he opened her wounds
with love
true love
with true love and gentleness
with humor and meaningful dialect
unafraid of what he found
the poison that had been sewn deep within her
didn't scare him
and while he acknowledged the ropes of venom
he reminded her that underneath the venom was her beauty
he reminded her that these ropes were not her
but simply recollections of them, of experiences
and the hurt this cold world has caused her
simply recollections of those that crossed her

Smehow he still saw her
underneath the ice cold barrier,
messy canvas,
wolf skin,
and unhealed wounds
he saw her
and he loved her

and for that she taught him how to be a better king
he called her the most beautiful minded woman he knew
and called her queen

1.4 him

It's just writing
mentally conflicted, secretly tormented between what is
what isn't
what was
what has been
letters about love,
letters about children
letters concerning lyrics and positions that simply shouldn't be written
They're just words
Sucking each other in just to let each other go
taking selfishness to another level
attempting to feed egos with necessary antidotes
trips to the dark side made 'em feel alive, down for the ride
for when it was bright it'd lead them to another side
a side they hadn't known before the ride
a side that brought better days and unexplainable highs
ones that if their better halves knew were such a prize
they'd die inside
a connection that neither you and I
could relate to

It's just letters
it's just typing
it's just text
it's just reading
it ain't sex
in the end, you can bet
they both leave with tons of regrets, years of memories they won't forget
for the greater good? Words left unsaid
but let's just pretend it never happened
three words three syllables
but it's just text
one word four letters
but it ain't sex
it never happened
it's just text

Scarlette's Song

2.0 It's Complicated

She hangs up the phone
The thought of him sickens her.
She rushes to the bathroom and locks the door.
Sinking to the bottom of the white floor, Scarlette repeats in her head,
"It's not real.
It never happened.
It doesn't exist."
Tormented by thoughts so dark, so cold,
so hot
so wrong
so passionate
Her heart's racing and her is mind focused on a million wrong things at once
"No Scar," she whispered to herself.
She took a deep breath.
She thought of Kair's encouraging words to her and said,
"This isn't my path, this isn't for me. My time is valuable, my heart is strong, and my mental space is fucking valuable, too. I am Scar, I heal wounds, wounds are not left on me."

She leaves the bathroom stall and heads back to her desk.
The 13 dozen of red roses that arrived the day before glowered back at her, tarnished.
Guilt filled the insides of her stomach.
She sat up straight, fixed her neatly made pony tail, ran her 'Envy' red lip stick across her full lips, and carefully placed the pair of solid, black frames back on her face.
"Clarity.
Peace.
Forgiveness," she repeated
Three trips to the trash later
The flowers were gone and she was back
What once was dark appeared light again
She was back.
he was gone, they were gone, it was gone, and she was back.

<u>Scarlette's Pieces</u>

1.5

The time with you was mesmerizing
Covered in you
Parts of you that I couldn't wash off even if I tried
Like a dove covered in oil
I was slowly dying, suffocating
But loved every single bit of it
Couldn't leave it
Could breathe without it
It was love, it was a drug
"I'm addicted Scar"
Words I use to revel in
Knowing I had against all odds captured a piece of your heart
The part you deemed unavailable to me
I laughed at your suffering
At your lack of control
Poison poured from my lungs and into yours
I laughed at your addiction
Unaware that soon I'd too fall victim
Victim to you
And would find myself lost, wading
And addicted too
Blissfully suffocating

1.6
They say confusion is a tool of the enemy
But in this case, I'm choosing to keep that tool close to me
Because it's the only thing that keeps you away from me
And really
Me away from you
So I'd rather stay here confused
I'd rather be hurt and filled with incomplete thoughts smothered
In words that don't make sense
Run-on sentences and words that won't allow me to convince or
Sway
And to my dismay,
Words that won't allow me explain.
And as a person that believes words actually have weight
It kills me to disable my ability to clearly and logically explain
How I'm feeling or what I'd like to say
I need it to not make sense
I need it to hurt even if no hurt exists
Even if your actions were completely unintentional, I'll hold on to
It
In order to let go of us
Going against everything I believe to let go of us
I'll cry and scream and blame it all on you
'Cause I know it's something you respond poorly to and I know
You'll not know what to do
Your lack of response will only add to
My hurt
Because I am but I'm not ready for this chapter to be through
But I need it to
You need it too.
Smooth out of options on how to be done with you,
But here's option 122.

1.7

How large of a flame beneath her seat will be needed
To muster up enough courage
To save she,
From she

1.8
It won't be perfect
There will be pieces broken
Dreams shattered
Choking
On the smoke required to burn the parts of you
That continue to hold you back
No partial will be offered
He wants it all and He wants you whole
But it will all be beautiful

1.9 Inner Thoughts

The room's a brewing

You're forced to face them

With nowhere to go

No one to come

No one to show and tell

All of the things you've worked so hard to get

Forced to go below the surface

Forced to look within

Cabin fever

2.0

Turn your head to the sky bright eyes
And when you're down
Be sure to surround
Yourself with loves that will remind you to
Turn your head to the sky

1

2.1

Out of a puddle of oil
She emerged
No longer submerged by the darkness that wished to keep her
Covered and under the dark waters of pretty things
Diamond rings, and emptiness
Now facing the light
The light that would ignite her soul
That would create her glow
That would require that she no longer had to seduce a soul, place,
Or thing into wanting her, into keeping her
They would eventually naturally flee to her
But for now it was bleak
But she was strong
And she'd keep pulling
She'd keep pushing
She'd keep fighting
For she knew that inside her was a
Light that evil had spent many years trying to fight
Through guilt and shame and selfishness and blame and relying
Upon man after man to keep her sane
Not realizing that this oil of her past,
Would only contribute to a bigger flame

A flame that would grow indefinitely and spread across many
Other beautiful flowers submerged in the very same oil
Ignite
Uncontrollable
Unstoppable
Never fully returning to that dark place
Full of fire, full of light, full of love

34208885R00064

Made in the USA
Middletown, DE
12 August 2016